FIRE STATIONS

by Emma Bassier

Cody Koala
An Imprint of Pop!
popbooksonline.com

abdobooks.com
Published by Pop!, a division of ABDO, PO Box 398166, Minneapolis, Minnesota 55439.

Printed in the United States of America, North Mankato, Minnesota

052019
092019

THIS BOOK CONTAINS RECYCLED MATERIALS

Cover Photo: iStockphoto
Interior Photos: iStockphoto, 5, 7 (top), 7 (bottom left), 7 (bottom right), 9, 10–11, 12, 14, 15, 17 (top left), 17 (top right), 17 (bottom), 19 (top), 19 (bottom left), 19 (bottom right), 20

Editor: Meg Gaertner
Series Designer: Jake Slavik

Library of Congress Control Number: 2018964597

Publisher's Cataloging-in-Publication Data

Names: Bassier, Emma, author.
Title: Fire stations / by Emma Bassier.
Description: Minneapolis, Minnesota : Pop!, 2020 | Series: Places in my community | Includes online resources and index.
Identifiers: ISBN 9781532163470 (lib. bdg.) | ISBN 9781532164910 (ebook)
Subjects: LCSH: Fire stations--Juvenile literature. | Firehouses--Juvenile literature. | Fire departments--Juvenile literature.
Classification: DDC 628.9--dc23

Hello! My name is

Cody Koala

Pop open this book and you'll find QR codes like this one, loaded with information, so you can learn even more!

Scan this code* and others like it while you read, or visit the website below to make this book pop.

popbooksonline.com/fire-stations

*Scanning QR codes requires a web-enabled smart device with a QR code reader app and a camera.

Table of Contents

Chapter 1

Red Fire Engine

Brrring! A bell goes off at the fire station. It means there is a fire somewhere. **Firefighters** jump into a **fire engine**. They are going to fight a fire.

Watch a video here!

Chapter 2

A Place That Protects

A fire station is a place that protects. Sometimes people need help right away. **Firefighters** respond to these emergencies. They put out fires and give **medical** care.

Watch a video here!

Chapter 3

Inside a Fire Station

A fire station has many areas. The biggest area is for storing the vehicles. A fire station has one or more **fire engines**. It may also have an **ambulance**.

Learn more here!

This vehicle room is large. It has several huge doors. Fire engines can quickly leave the station.

Firefighters keep their vehicles clean. They make sure the vehicles have the right **supplies**.

Fire stations have areas for storing **gear** and tools. Gear includes the clothing firefighters wear to stay safe. It includes **fire extinguishers** and **medical** supplies.

Fire stations receive more calls for medical help than for firefighting.

Firefighters live at the fire station for periods of time. The station has bedrooms.

Firefighters can sleep there. The station also has a kitchen and eating area.

Firefighters keep learning more about how to fight fires. They also train to stay strong. A fire station has classrooms. It has rooms where firefighters can work out.

fire extinguisher

first aid supplies

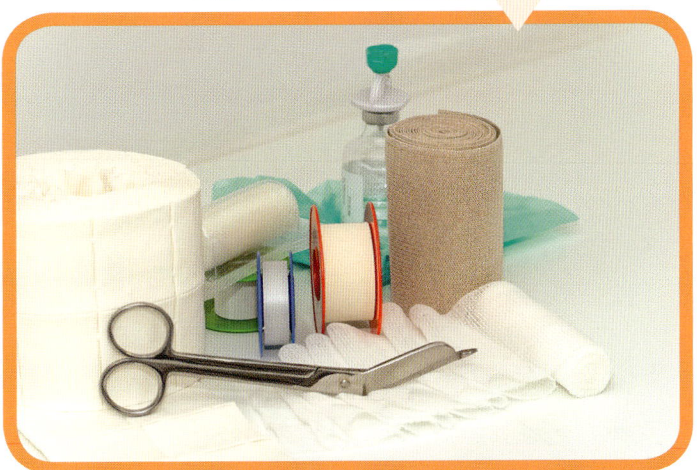

ambulance

Chapter 4

Keeping People Safe

Fire stations are important to the community. People know they can call for help. They will receive help quickly.

Learn more here!

Big cities have several fire stations. These stations help the community. **Firefighters** do not have to drive as far when responding to a call.

Firefighters try to leave the station within one minute of receiving the call.

Making Connections

Text-to-Self

Have you ever visited a fire station? Would you like to? Why or why not?

Text-to-Text

Have you read a book about another place in the community? How is that place similar to or different from a fire station?

Text-to-World

Firefighters help people. What other jobs can people do to help others?

Glossary

ambulance – a vehicle that gives people medical care while taking them to a hospital.

fire engine – a truck used by firefighters to carry their tools and fight fires.

fire extinguisher – a tool people use to put out fires.

firefighter – a person who puts out fires and responds to emergencies.

gear – tools used for a specific job.

medical – having to do with doctors or medicine.

supplies – things that people use to do a task.

Index

Online Resources

popbooksonline.com

Thanks for reading this Cody Koala book!

Scan this code* and others like it in this book, or visit the website below to make this book pop!

popbooksonline.com/fire-stations

*Scanning QR codes requires a web-enabled smart device with a QR code reader app and a camera.